A Note From Rick Renner

I am on a personal quest to see a "revival of the Bible" so people can establish their lives on a firm foundation that will stand strong and endure the test when the end-time storm winds begin to intensify.

In order to experience a revival of the Bible in your personal life, it is important to take time each day to read, receive, and apply its truths to your life. James tells us that if we will continue in the perfect law of liberty — refusing to be forgetful hearers but determined to be doers — we will be blessed in our ways. As you watch or listen to the programs in this series and work through this corresponding study guide, I trust that you will search the Scriptures and allow the Holy Spirit to help you hear something new from God's Word that applies specifically to your life. I encourage you to be a doer of the Word that He reveals to you. Whatever the cost, I assure you — it will be worth it.

> Thy words were found, and I did eat them;
> and thy word was unto me the joy and rejoicing of mine heart:
> for I am called by thy name, O Lord God of hosts.
> — Jeremiah 15:16

Your brother and friend in Jesus Christ,

Rick Renner

Trick or Treat: A Christian Response to Halloween

Copyright © 2020 by Rick Renner
8316 E. 73rd St.
Tulsa, Oklahoma 74133

Published by Rick Renner Ministries
www.renner.org

ISBN 13: 978-1-68031-800-5

eBook ISBN 13: 978-1-68031-801-2

How To Use This Study Guide

This five-lesson study guide corresponds to *"Trick or Treat: A Christian Response to Halloween" With Rick Renner* (Renner TV). Each lesson in this study guide covers a topic that is addressed during the program series, with questions and references supplied to draw you deeper into your own private study of the Scriptures on this subject.

To derive the most benefit from this study guide, consider the following:

First, watch or listen to the program prior to working through the corresponding lesson in this guide. (Programs can also be viewed at **renner.org** by clicking on the Media/Archives links.)

Second, take the time to look up the scriptures included in each lesson. Prayerfully consider their application to your own life.

Third, use a journal or notebook to make note of your answers to each lesson's Study Questions and Practical Application challenges.

Fourth, invest specific time in prayer and in the Word of God to consult with the Holy Spirit. Write down the scriptures or insights He reveals to you.

Finally, take action! Whatever the Lord tells you to do according to His Word, do it.

For added insights on this subject, it is recommended that you obtain Rick Renner's book *Dressed to Kill: A Biblical Approach to Spiritual Warfare and Armor.* You may also select from Rick's other available resources by placing your order at **renner.org** or by calling 1-800-742-5593.

TOPIC

Is the Devil Funny?

SCRIPTURES

1. **John 10:10** — The thief cometh not, but for to steal, and to kill, and to destroy: I am come that they might have life, and that they might have it more abundantly.

2. **1 Peter 5:9** — Whom resist stedfast in the faith...

GREEK WORDS

1. "thief" — **κλέπτης** (*kleptes*): a bandit, thief, pickpocket, or scam artist; where we get the word "kleptomaniac"

2. "steal" — **κλέπτω** (*klepto*): pictures one so artful in the way he steals that his exploits of thievery are nearly undetectable; a scam artist or pickpocket; where we get the word "kleptomaniac"

3. "kill" — **θύω** (*thuo*): not to kill, as in murder, but to sacrifice; to surrender or to give up something that is precious and dear; used among the Greeks when they sacrificed to their gods — or even among the Jews when they sacrificed something to God

4. "destroy" — **ἀπόλλυμι** (*apollumi*): to ruin, waste, trash, devastate, or destroy; same root word for "unloose" used in Luke 3:16 when John the Baptist said of Jesus, "...But one mightier than I cometh, the latchet of whose shoes I am not worthy to unloose..."; describes something that is ruined, unraveled, undone, devastated, trashed, destroyed, or completely liquidated

5. "that" — **ἵνα** (*hina*): in order that; expresses explicit purpose

6. "might have" — **ἔχωσιν** (*echosin*): future, plural form of **ἔχω** (*echo*); to have, hold, or possess

7. "life" — **ζωή** (*zoe*): life filled with zest and vitality

8. "more abundantly" — **περισσός** (*perissos*): abundantly; excessively; exceedingly; extraordinarily; something that abounds in an extraordinary measure; so profuse that it can be likened to a river overflowing and flooding beyond its banks; overflowing, plentiful, or even superabundant

SYNOPSIS

The five lessons in this study on *Trick or Treat: A Christian Response to Halloween* will focus on the following topics:

- Is the Devil Funny?
- How Did Early Christians Respond to Pagan Celebrations?
- Is Halloween for You?
- The History of Halloween
- How Should You Respond to Halloween?

The emphasis of this lesson:

There is nothing funny about the devil. He was and is a thief and murderer bent on destruction. We shouldn't have anything to do with him, nor should we participate in pagan holidays like Halloween that celebrates the death and decay he produces.

One of the seven wonders of the ancient world was the great Temple of Artemis located in the city of Ephesus. In that temple, 6,000 pagan priests and priestesses served, and people came from all over the world to worship this idolatrous deity. Artemis — also known as Diana, the Latin name for Artemis — was worshiped throughout the Roman and Greek-speaking worlds and had two distinct forms. There was a western version, where her image appeared to be a huntress; and there was an Asian version, in which Diana looked like she was covered with multiple breasts. However, they were not breasts; they were actually bulls' testicles, which is a symbol of fertility. Clearly, the worship of Diana (or Artemis) was a very dark, devious religion.

When the Church was established in Ephesus and people began surrendering their lives to the lordship of Christ, many were delivered from demonic influences, including the pagan worship of Artemis. These Early Christians did not believe the devil was funny. On the contrary, they knew that he and his demons were a serious force to be reckoned with and wanted nothing to do with him.

In the same way, we need to take the devil seriously, which includes disconnecting from the evil practices of this world that expose us to dangerous demonic activity. This brings us to a very important question: Should Christians be celebrating Halloween? Is it just a fun, harmless event, or is there something more sinister than we realize brewing beneath the surface of which we need to be aware?

The Devil Is a 'Thief'

No one knew the character of the devil better than Jesus. In John 10:10, He described the devil's mode of operation, saying, "The thief cometh not, but for to steal, and to kill, and to destroy…." First, notice that Jesus called the devil a "thief." In Greek, the word "thief" is *kleptes*, which describes *a bandit, thief, pickpocket, or scam artist*. It is from where we get the term "kleptomaniac."

By using this word *kleptes*, Jesus was saying, "Don't be surprised. The devil can't help himself. He is flawed, defective, and twisted. From the very beginning of time, he has been a thief. Something in him is bound and determined that he must try to take what belongs to someone else."

The first appearance of Satan in the Old Testament depicts him lusting after the throne of God. He wanted the adoration of the angels and the geographical location of God's throne on the sides of the north. But God — knowing the evil iniquity growing in Lucifer's heart — cast him out of Heaven because of his pompous pride (*see* Isaiah 14:12-15).

The next time the devil appears is in the Garden of Eden. Genesis 3 records that he worked through the serpent to successfully steal Adam's position of authority over the earth. Ever since then he has been scamming mankind out of anything and everything he can get.

It's His Nature To 'Steal'

As the chief thief in the universe, Satan is always looking to "steal" whatever he can from whomever he can. The word "steal" in John 10:10 is the Greek word *klepto*, which is from the same root of the word *kleptes*. It describes *one so artful in the way he steals that his exploits of thievery are nearly undetectable; a scam artist or pickpocket*. Again, it is from where we get the word "kleptomaniac."

Basically, when Jesus said, "The thief cometh not, but for to steal," He was saying, "The kleptomaniac, when he shows up, will begin to behave like a kleptomaniac. He can't restrain himself. He'll steal, steal, steal because it is his nature to steal." He doesn't take things because he needs them; he steals because it is in his nature.

The truth is an attack from the enemy may not even be about you. He just wants what you have because it's his twisted nature to steal. If you're healthy, he wants your health. If you're married, he wants your marriage. If you've got a good job, he wants your job. If you've got kids, he wants your kids. It doesn't even matter what it is; he just wants whatever is yours. The devil is a *kleptes* — *a bandit, a thief,* or *a scam artist; one so artful in the way he steals that his exploits of thievery are nearly undetectable; a pickpocket.* When he shows up, he'll begin — very artfully and seductively — trying to take everything you have.

He Also Comes To 'Kill'

What else does the devil attempt to do in our lives? Jesus said he also comes to "kill." Most people mistake the word "kill" in John 10:10 to mean slaughter, massacre, bloodshed, or murder. But that is not the case. In Greek, the word "kill" is *thuo,* which doesn't mean kill, as in murder, but *to sacrifice.* It carries the idea of *surrendering or giving up something that is precious and dear.* This word was used among the Greeks when they sacrificed to their gods — or even among the Jews when they sacrificed something to God.

By using the word *thuo* — translated here as "kill" — Jesus is teaching us that the devil can disguise himself to sound religious. Sometimes he can even sound like God. Remember when he came against Jesus in the wilderness? The devil quoted Scripture to Jesus in an effort to get Him to give into temptation. But Jesus rejected the enemy's twisted version of God's Word and countered his lies with truth.

This lets us know that if we have anything left after the devil has stolen from us, he may try to speak to us in religious terms to get us to surrender it to him. He'll say things like, "You know what? There's no hope of recovery. There's no way you'll ever be able to restore what you've lost. Why try to believe? Just lay it all on the altar. You might as well give it up. Just sacrifice it and walk away."

Friend, the devil is out to steal and to kill. He wants you to lay down your promises, your dreams, and everything you hold dear so that he can continue to expand and bring to life his evil schemes to devastate and obliterate you.

Satan Also 'Destroys' Whatever He Can

Again, Jesus said, "The thief cometh not, but for to steal, and to kill, and to destroy..." (John 10:10). The word "destroy" here is the Greek word *apollumi*, which means *to ruin, waste, trash, devastate, or destroy*. It describes *something that is ruined, unraveled, undone, devastated, trashed, destroyed, or completely liquidated*. It is the same root word for "unloose" used in Luke 3:16 when John the Baptist said of Jesus, "...But one mightier than I cometh, the latchet of whose shoes I am not worthy to unloose...."

Think about it. What happened when a person living in the First Century "unloosed" their shoes? One leather strap at a time was released until their shoes would begin to completely unravel and fall apart. Jesus' use of this word *apollumi* — translated here as "destroy" — tells us that after the devil steals from you and coaxes you into sacrificing all your hopes and dreams, he will continue to attack you until you are completely unraveled and undone.

Taking into account the meaning of all these words, here is the *Renner Interpretive Version (RIV)* of the first part of John 10:10:

> **The thief wants to get his hands into every good thing in your life. In fact, this pickpocket is looking for any opportunity to wiggle his way so deeply into your personal affairs that he can walk off with everything you hold precious and dear. And that's not all. When he's finished stealing all your goods and possessions, he'll take his plan to rob you blind to the next level by creating conditions and situations so horrible that you'll see no way to solve the problems except to sacrifice everything that remains from previous attacks. The goal of this thief is to totally devastate your life. If nothing stops him, he'll leave you insolvent, flat broke, and cleaned out in every area of your life. You'll end up feeling as if you're finished and out of business. Make no mistake. The enemy's ultimate aim is to obliterate you...**

Jesus Came To Give You Abundant Life!

After Jesus informed us of how the devil operates, He then told us how *He* operates. He said, "The thief cometh not, but for to steal, and to kill, and to destroy: I am come that they might have life, and that they might have it more abundantly" (John 10:10).

When Jesus said, "…I am come that," the Greek word for "that" is *hina*, which means *in order that*. It expresses *explicit purpose*. Jesus said He explicitly came that "…they might have life…" (John 10:10). In Greek, the words "might have" is the word *echosin*, which is the future, plural form of the word *echo*, meaning *to have, hold, or possess*. Jesus' purpose in coming was that we might *have*, might *hold*, and we might truly *possess* "life." The word "life" is the Greek word *zoe*, which describes *life filled with zest and vitality*.

Now this is not just a mediocre form of life. It is life "more abundantly," which is the Greek word *perissos*, and it means *abundantly, excessively, exceedingly, extraordinary*. It is *something that abounds in an extraordinary measure* and is so profuse that it can be likened to a river overflowing and flooding beyond its banks. It carries the idea of *overflowing, plentiful*, or even *superabundant*.

Taking into account the meaning of all these words, here is the *Renner Interpretive Version (RIV)* of the second part of John 10:10:

> **But I have specifically come with the express purpose that you will have, hold, and possess a phenomenal and amazing life. My purpose is that you will possess life so full that it overflows and spills over like a mighty river so full of water that its banks can no longer contain it all. I'm talking about an amazingly full, spirited, and vivacious life that is literally overflowing and spilling over. I have explicitly come so you can possess an abundant, profuse, plentiful, and bountiful life.**

Friend, that is what Jesus came to give *you*! Through Him you can experience a life that is so overflowing with His goodness it can hardly be put into words.

When we pull together the meanings of all these words, here is the complete *Renner Interpretive Version (RIV)* of John 10:10:

> **The thief wants to get his hands into every good thing in your life. In fact, this pickpocket is looking for any opportunity to wiggle his way so deeply into your personal affairs that he can walk off with everything you hold precious and dear. And that's not all. When he's finished stealing all your goods and possessions, he'll take his plan to rob you blind to the next level by creating conditions and situations so horrible that you'll**

see no way to solve the problems except to sacrifice everything that remains from previous attacks. The goal of this thief is to totally devastate your life. If nothing stops him, he'll leave you insolvent, flat broke, and cleaned out in every area of your life. You'll end up feeling as if you're finished and out of business. Make no mistake. The enemy's ultimate aim is to obliterate you. But I have specifically come with the express purpose that you will have, hold, and possess a phenomenal and amazing life. My purpose is that you will possess life so full that it overflows and spills over like a mighty river so full of water that its banks can no longer contain it all. I'm talking about an amazingly full, spirited, and vivacious life that is literally overflowing and spilling over. I have explicitly come so you can possess an abundant, profuse, plentiful, and bountiful life.

In our next lesson, we will look at how First-Century believers responded to pagan celebrations and see how we can apply their example in our own lives.

STUDY QUESTIONS

Study to shew thyself approved unto God, a workman that needeth not to be ashamed, rightly dividing the word of truth.
— 2 Timothy 2:15

1. Carefully reread the original Greek meanings of the words "steal," "kill," and "destroy" in John 10:10. What new insights is the Holy Spirit showing you about the devil's mode of operation that you have never seen before? What's your most impactful takeaway from this passage? Why?

2. According to First John 3:8, John 10:10, and Luke 19:10 what are the primary reasons Jesus came to earth? How would you say your life is benefiting from His finished work on the cross?

PRACTICAL APPLICATION

But be ye doers of the word, and not hearers only, deceiving your own selves.
— James 1:22

1. Jesus said that Satan is a "thief" that comes to "steal." He wants what you have because it's his twisted nature to steal. What good things in your life has Satan been avidly trying to steal?

2. In Greek, the word "kill" is *thuo*, which means *to sacrifice*. It carries the idea of *surrendering or giving up something that is precious and dear.* What dreams and promises from God is the enemy trying to get you to lay down and sacrifice? Pray and ask God for strength to stand your ground and not sacrifice another thing.

3. Jesus said, "…I am come that they might have life, and that they might have it more abundantly" (John 10:10). In what areas of your life are you experiencing the abundant, overflowing life of vitality that Jesus promised? Take time now to thank Him for His love, His mercy, and His blessing.

LESSON 2

TOPIC

How Did Early Christians Respond to Pagan Celebrations?

SCRIPTURES

1. **1 John 5:21** — Little children, keep yourselves from idols. Amen.

2. **1 Corinthians 10:14,19-21** — Wherefore, my dearly beloved, flee from idolatry…. What say I then? That the idol is any thing, or that which is offered in sacrifice to idols is any thing? But I say, that the things which the Gentiles sacrifice, they sacrifice to devils, and not to God: and I would not that ye should have fellowship with devils. Ye cannot drink the cup of the Lord, and the cup of devils: ye cannot be partakers of the Lord's table, and the table of devils.

3. **1 John 4:4** — …Greater is he that is in you, than he that is in the world.

GREEK WORDS

1. "keep" — **φυλάσσω** (*phulasso*): to save, protect, preserve, or to guard; pictures a military guard; in history, depicted the uninterrupted

vigilance that shepherds showed in keeping their flocks; also used to depict a military guard who exercised unbroken vigilance; to guard, protect, secure, shield, or watch over in order to protect one from some outside foul force

2. "from" — ἀπό (*apo*): from; away from; implies intentional distance

3. "idols" — εἴδωλον (*eidolon*): plural, idols of false gods

4. "flee" — φεύγω (*pheugo*): to flee; to take flight; to run away; to run hastily; to run as fast as possible, or to escape; pictures one's feet flying as he runs from a situation

5. "devils" — δαιμόνιον (*daimonion*): evil spirits; demons; devils; ancient world generally believed demons thickly populated the lower regions of the air and that these spirits were the primary cause of disasters and suffering in the earth; could depict a person deemed insane; depicts those possessed with evil spirits, who suffered spirit-inflicted mental or physical infirmities; supernatural beings; superhuman forces; or spirits that could be conjured up by magic, incantations, or special rituals

6. "that ye should" — γίνομαι (*ginomai*): something that develops or evolves over a period of time; denotes something that comes into existence over the passage of time

7. "fellowship" — κοινωνός (*koinonos*): plural form of κοινός (*koinos*); that which is common or mutually shared, such as property that jointly belongs to two or more people; but when κοινός (*koinos*) develops into the word κοινωνός (*koinonos*), it refers specifically to the ideas of engagement, involvement, fellowship, or participation

8. "amen" — ἀμήν (*amen*): amen; so let it be; an emphasis marker used to emphasize a statement of great importance

SYNOPSIS

As we saw in our first lesson, the legendary Temple of Artemis was located in the ancient city of Ephesus, and its structure was simply massive. It had 127 columns that were each 60 feet tall, and at the building's peak, it towered 110 feet into the air. There were 6,000 priests and priestesses who served in the Temple of Artemis 24 hours a day, 7 days a week, and people came from all around the world to worship this Greek goddess of fertility.

Before surrendering their lives to Christ, many believers in the Early Church participated in the pagan practices that took place in the Temple of Artemis. Once saved, they shunned places like these because they were filled with demonic activity. They knew that the devil and his demons are real and they wanted nothing to do with them.

As believers, we are called to follow this example and *flee* from all forms of idolatry and pagan festivities — including participating in Halloween. The reality is Halloween is no laughing matter; it is a celebration that glorifies death and invites demonic activity. When the rest of the world is trick-or-treating and being scared out of their wits, Christians should refrain from engaging in such pagan practices.

The emphasis of this lesson:

Believers in the Early Church were instructed to flee from all idolatry and refrain from having fellowship with demons, and the same is true for us. Participating in pagan practices exposes us to demonic-infested environments that are detrimental to our spiritual health.

Toward the end of the First Century, the apostle John was imprisoned on the isle of Patmos for his faith in Christ. It was in a cave on this island that Jesus appeared to John and spoke to him about the seven major churches on the continent of Asia. He expressed great concern because many believers in these churches were flirting with the world and compromising their convictions by participating in pagan practices and idolatry.

For example, Christ rebuked the churches in Ephesus and Pergamum for their tolerance of the Nicolaitans — a group who advocated worldly compromise in order to avoid being persecuted by pagans. Likewise, Christ rebuked the congregation at Thyatira for a flirtatious attitude with idolatry. They were allowing a woman named Jezebel to teach believers to mix and mingle with the unsaved people in the community and engage in pagan practices in hopes of being accepted.

Jesus was against any willingness to compromise and assimilate with pagan culture. The situation had progressed to such a point that believers were even willing to embrace idolatry alongside their worship of Christ. When John was released from Patmos, he returned to the city of Ephesus and wrote the gospel of John as well as First, Second, and Third John. Clearly, the words of Jesus had penetrated deeply into John's heart, which prompted him to write the powerful charge recorded in First John 5:21: "Little children, keep yourselves from idols. Amen."

What It Means To 'Keep Yourself From Idols'

There is much we can gain from understanding the original Greek used in First John 5:21, starting with the meaning of the word "keep." In Greek, the word "keep" is *phulasso*, and it means *to save, protect, preserve, or to guard oneself from something*. It depicts *a military guard who exercised unbroken vigilance*. Moreover, it pictures *the uninterrupted vigilance shepherds showed in keeping their flocks*. It carries the idea *to guard, protect, secure, shield, or watch over in order to protect one from some outside foul force*.

The word *phulasso* occurs at least 400 times in the Old Testament Septuagint and 31 times in the New Testament. Because of its frequent use, there is no doubt about its meaning. It describes the *guarding* and *protection* of a thing, such as the guarding of a house, property, possessions, or even graves, and it denotes the *alertness* and *sleeplessness* of the person who is *on guard*.

The word *phulasso* could also imply the *safekeeping* of something entrusted to someone, and it was often used in a military sense to describe a *garrison* or *a guard*. To "keep" (*phulasso*) something demanded that a person be loyal to the task — never lethargic or lackadaisical. If that individual "fell asleep on the job," the consequences could be grave. Therefore, he must be on *full alert* at all times.

The tense of the word *phulasso* — translated here as "keep" — doesn't refer to a temporary alertness, but rather a lifelong determination to remain wide-awake and on course to the very end. John's use of this word in First John 5:21 conveys that we are to defend ourselves against the evil that is always lurking in the shadows — just waiting for us to drop our guard. Like a garrison defends a strategic position, God has called us to defend and be the guards of our lives.

When John commanded his readers to "...keep yourself from idols," he was urging them to stay *on alert* regarding the danger of idolatry. The word "from" here is the Greek word *apo*, meaning *from* or *away from*, and it implies *intentional distance*. Thus, John said, "Be very intentional about putting space between you and idols." The word "idols" in Greek is the word *eidolon*, which is plural and refers to *idols of false gods*.

Clearly, idolatry and its insidious effects were so detrimental that believers needed to continually stay alert in order to remain free from its contaminating influences. It was absolutely essential that they stood firm and refused to compromise. The same holds true for believers today.

We Are To 'Flee' From Idolatry

The apostle Paul also commented on idolatry and pagan celebrations. His words in First Corinthians 10:14 are a perfect example. He said, "Wherefore, my dearly beloved, flee from idolatry." What is interesting is that Paul taught that an idol was nothing more than a man-made object, completely devoid of power. At the same time, he urged believers to flee from them. He clarified his instruction by saying:

> **"What say I then? That the idol is any thing, or that which is offered to idols is any thing? But I say, that the things which the Gentiles sacrifice, they sacrifice to devils, and not to God; and I would not that ye should have fellowship with devils. Ye cannot drink the cup of the Lord, and the cup of devils: ye cannot be partakers of the Lord's table, and the table of devils."**
> **1 Corinthians 10:19-21**

In this passage, Paul affirms that idols are really nothing but lifeless stone and wood. However, while the physical idol itself had no power, the environment of the pagan temple where pagan celebrations were taking place was filled with evil demonic activity. He didn't want believers going into such places and walking out under the influence of demons. That is precisely why Paul strongly urged believers to "flee from idolatry."

The word "flee" in First Corinthians 10:14 is the Greek word *pheugo*, which means *to flee, to take flight, to run away, to run hastily, to run as fast as possible, or to escape*. It pictures one's feet flying as he runs from a situation. The tense used here conveys they were to *constantly flee* from idolatry with no exception. Paul was emphatically stating that idolatry and pagan celebrations were so fatal, they should never be tolerated under any circumstances — *not then, not now, not ever*. Although an idol by itself is nothing, the environment in which idolatry was practiced is *permeated* with demonic activity.

Fleeing Evil Environments
Reduces Exposure to Demonic Influences

Looking once again at First Corinthians 10:20, Paul said, "But I say, that the things which the Gentiles sacrifice, they sacrifice to devils, and not to God; and I would not that ye should have fellowship with devils."

Here Paul used the word "devils" twice. It is the Greek word *daimonion*, which describes *evil spirits, demons, or devils*. People in the ancient world generally believed demons thickly populated the lower regions of the air and that these spirits were the primary cause of disasters and suffering in the earth. The word *daimonion* could also depict *a person deemed insane* or *those possessed with evil spirits, who suffered spirit-inflicted mental or physical infirmities*. Moreover, it denotes *supernatural beings, superhuman forces, or spirits that could be conjured up by magic, incantations, or special rituals*.

In the era of the early New Testament, it was very hard to escape a pagan environment because the world was saturated with paganism. For example, if you would have entered the city of Ephesus in the First Century, you would have seen one pagan temple after another. If you traveled north to the city of Smyrna, you would have seen the same thing. In fact, this devious, dark idolatry was prevalent in the cities of Pergamum, Thyatira, Sardis, Laodicea, Athens, and Corinth. Hence, it was virtually impossible to live in the First Century without living near a pagan temple.

In the dark environment of pagan temples, the spirit realm could be stirred up resulting in tangible manifestations of dark, supernatural power. It was for this reason that Paul urged believers "to flee" from environments where works of darkness were practiced. The Bible stresses that we have no reason to fear demon spirits because Christ has overcome the darkness. But fleeing evil is a biblical command because it is foolish to put ourselves at risk in a demonic environment.

Now someone might say, "Well, the Bible says in First John, 'Greater is he that is in you than he that is in the world,' so it won't hurt us to go to such places." But that is not necessarily true. We need to use the wisdom God has given us. Although we may not fall off the edge of a cliff by simply standing near it, playing around the cliff's edge greatly increases the danger of slipping. Keeping a "safe distance" from the edge assures that we will *not* slip and fall. Yes, "Greater is he that is in you than he that is in the world" (1 John 4:4), but the same person who wrote this verse also told us just a few verses later, "Little children, keep yourselves from idols" (1 John 5:21).

To Flourish in God's Light
We Must Stop Flirting With Darkness

Notice what Paul said in the second part of First Corinthians 10:20: "…I would not that ye should have fellowship with devils." The phrase "that ye should" is the future form of the Greek word *ginomai*, which describes *something that develops or evolves over a period of time*. It denotes *something that comes into existence over the passage of time*. By using the word *ginomai* — translated here as "that ye should" — Paul is saying that by being in the wrong spiritual environment, over time a person can gradually become affected by it. In early New Testament times, Paul said that when people sacrificed to idols, they put themselves in jeopardy of becoming engaged with demons. He declared a person's physical proximity to idol worship potentially puts him or her in position to come under the influence of demons. There is great potential spiritual damage that people can subject themselves to by simply being in a wrong spiritual environment.

This brings us to the word "fellowship" — the Greek word *koinono*, which is the plural form of *koinos*, and it describes *that which is common or mutually shared*, such as property that jointly belongs to two or more people. But when *koinos* develops into the word *koinonos*, it refers specifically to *the ideas of engagement, involvement, fellowship, or participation*.

So when Paul used this word *koinonos* in the context of demons, this literally meant that he didn't want his audience to become *engaged*, *involved*, or *partners* with demons as a result of their proximity to idolatrous practices. This verse sounds a screaming alarm that those who offer sacrifices at pagan altars or attend pagan feasts potentially make themselves susceptible to coming under a demonic influence of some sort — even to the point of becoming *partners* with demons.

Pulling together the meanings of these words, here is the *Renner Interpretive Version (RIV)* of the second part of First Corinthians 10:20:

> **...And I would not that ye should have participation with devils [as a result of being in the atmosphere of idolatrous sacrifices and activities].**

It is impossible to exaggerate the role that pagan temples and idols played in the ancient world. Most cities were built around temples and embraced the multitude of pagan cults. Magic, incantations, amulets, charms, sacrifices, rituals, pagan festivals — all of these were a part of life for all pagans. So living in close quarters with the demonic realm was a daily reality for every believer living in the First Century.

However, there is no record in the book of Acts of preachers, apostles, or believers attending pagan temples to meet people, advertise their messages, help them identify with local populations, or become more "seeker-friendly" to the unchurched. God called people out of those dark environments into His holy community. There was never an option to remain in both worlds. God called them *out of* darkness *into* His marvelous light (*see* First Peter 2:9). He knew that skirting around the edges of darkness was *not* the way for His children to flourish in His light. The same is true for us. Christ demands complete separation.

Intentionally Distance Yourself From Evil

What Paul declared in First Corinthians 10:14 is echoed by the apostle John in First John 5:21. He said, "Little children, keep yourselves from idols. Amen." Remember, the word "from" is the Greek word *apo*, which implies *intentional distance*. John was directing his readers to be very intentional about purposely placing distance between them and idols.

To this, he added the four-letter word "amen," which means *amen*; *so let it be*. It is *an emphasis marker, a word used to emphasize a statement of great importance*.

Taking into account the original Greek meanings of these words, here is the *Renner Interpretive Version (RIV)* of First John 5:21:

> **Little children, I immediately order you to withdraw from idols. Those idols — and what they represent — are so evil that you need to seriously guard yourself against them and stay away from them altogether. I'm leaving no wiggle room on this issue. I'm absolutely and emphatically ordering you to immediately put as much space as possible between yourself and idols. They are evil and represent a menace to your life, so you must urgently guard against them. What I'm telling you right now is not open for debate and is not optional. It is an order that I fully expect you to obey. In fact, to underscore the seriousness of what I am telling you, I'm even adding an "amen" to stress the point. I expect you to explicitly obey my instructions on this issue — and do it now!**

What Does All This Mean to Us Today?

During the month of October, people all over the world celebrate Halloween — including many Christians. They say, "There's no harm in participating in Halloween. Trick or treating is really no big deal." But that is not true. The fact is their involvement in the holiday is placing them in close proximity to demonic forces — just as the First-Century believers were exposed to demonic activity by entering pagan temples and engaging in pagan practices.

Friend, there are evil influences that we need to stay away from, and the spirits associated with Halloween is one of them. There is nothing beneficial about celebrating a day dedicated to death, the devil, and demonic spirits. In our next lesson, we are going to look at what the Bible explicitly has to say about Christians being involved in pagan celebrations.

STUDY QUESTIONS

Study to shew thyself approved unto God, a workman that needeth
not to be ashamed, rightly dividing the word of truth.
— 2 Timothy 2:15

1. In your own words, describe what you understand it means to "keep yourself from idols."
2. How is God's charge to *keep yourself* from idols in First John 5:21 similar to His instructions in Proverbs 4:23; Acts 15:29, First Timothy 5:22, and the last part of James 1:27?
3. According to Psalm 119:9 and Proverbs 4:20-27, what can you do to help keep yourself pure? (Also consider John 15:3; 17:17; Ephesians 5:26; and First Peter 1:22.)

PRACTICAL APPLICATION

But be ye doers of the word, and not hearers only,
deceiving your own selves.
— James 1:22

1. Evil is always lurking in the shadows — just waiting for us to drop our guard so it can gain entrance into our lives. Stop and think: What areas of your life does the enemy repeatedly try to gain access? These are areas where you seem to more easily fall into ungodly thinking or behavior.
2. Through Paul, the Holy Spirit instructed us to "...flee from idolatry" (1 Corinthians 10:14), because the environment in which idolatry is practiced is permeated with demonic activity. Pause and pray: *"Lord,*

are there any places I am going or anything I am exposing myself to that is making me vulnerable to the influence of demons? If so, where?"

3. What can you do differently to stay *on guard* and remain spiritually awake so that Satan doesn't get the upper hand (*see* 1 Peter 5:8)? How can you *intentionally put space* between you and those things that seem to be like idols in your life?

LESSON 3

TOPIC

Is Halloween for You?

SCRIPTURES

1. **1 John 5:21** — Little children, keep yourselves from idols. Amen.
2. **Acts 15:19,20** — Wherefore my sentence is, that we trouble not them, which from among the Gentiles are turned to God: but that we write unto them, that they abstain from pollutions of idols...

GREEK WORDS

1. "keep" — **φυλάσσω** (*phulasso*): to save, protect, preserve, or to guard; pictures a military guard; in history, depicted the uninterrupted vigilance shepherds showed in keeping their flocks; also used to depict a military guard who exercised unbroken vigilance; to guard, protect, secure, shield, or watch over in order to protect one from some outside foul force
2. "from" — **ἀπό** (*apo*): from; away from; implies intentional distance
3. "idols" — **εἴδωλον** (*eidolon*): plural, idols of false gods
4. "amen" — **ἀμήν** (*amen*): amen; so let it be; an emphasis marker used to emphasize a statement of great importance
5. "abstain from" — **ἀπέχομαι** (*apechomai*): to abstain; to withdraw from; to stay away from; to put distance between oneself and something else; to deliberately or intentionally refrain from something; to put physical distance between oneself and another person, place, or thing

6. "pollutions" — ἀλίσγημα (*alisgema*): depicts something that is defiled; makes it clear that idolatry has a spiritually polluting and contaminating effect

SYNOPSIS

In our two previous lessons, we learned that the city of Ephesus was home to the great Temple of Artemis. It was a colossal structure, featuring 127 columns that each rose 60 feet into the sky, and its peak was 110 feet in height. As one of the seven wonders of the ancient world, people came from everywhere to see this massive building and pay homage to Artemis, the goddess of fertility.

Inside the temple, 6,000 priests and priestesses served this dark, demonic religion. Every day as the eerie music played and poured into the surrounding streets, sacrifices were offered to Artemis and to the demonic spirits energizing her worship. Believers in the Early Church knew they needed to stay away from this spiritually depraved environment. In fact, the apostle Paul had said, "…I would not that ye should have fellowship with devils" (1 Corinthians 10:20). Paul knew that by hanging out in these places, believers would be subjecting themselves to a foul spiritual influence that would be detrimental to their spiritual well-being.

For us, this brings into question the pagan celebration of Halloween. Next to Christmas, it is one of the most celebrated holidays around the world. As Christians, should we participate in this pagan festival? Is God okay with us dressing up our children and grandchildren — and ourselves — in various costumes resembling skeletons, witches, and devils? What should be your response to Halloween?

The emphasis of this lesson:

The Early Church was taught the crucial importance of keeping themselves from idols. Although paganism abounded in the ancient world, believers learned how to 'abstain' from the pollutions of idolatry and the poisonous side-effects it produces. We would do well to hear and heed this same warning and abstain from participating in Halloween.

Keep Yourself From Idols

In our last lesson, we saw that Jesus appeared to the apostle John while he was imprisoned on the isle of Patmos, expressing His great concern about what was going on in the churches of Ephesus, Pergamum, Thyatira, Sardis, and Laodicea. Their compromise with the world and flirtation with idolatry had led to their acceptance of — and in some cases their participation in — various forms of pagan practices, which Jesus was vehemently against.

With Christ's rebuke fresh in his mind, John wrote First John 5:21, declaring, "Little children, keep yourselves from idols. Amen." The word "keep" is the Greek word *phulasso*, and it means *to save, protect, preserve, or to guard oneself from something*. It depicted *the uninterrupted vigilance shepherds showed in keeping their flocks*. Moreover, this word was used to depict *a military guard who exercised unbroken vigilance*. It carries the idea *to guard, to protect, to secure, to shield, or watch over in order to protect one from some outside foul force*.

The word *phulasso* occurs at least 400 times in the Old Testament Septuagint and 31 times in the New Testament. To "keep" (*phulasso*) something demanded that a person be loyal to the task — never lethargic or lackadaisical. And the tense of the word *phulasso* doesn't refer to a temporary alertness, but rather a lifelong determination to remain wide-awake and on course to the very end.

John's use of this word in the context of idolatry and pagan celebrations conveys that *we are to guard, to protect, to preserve, and to shield ourselves* from places and practices of idolatry. When John charged his readers to "...keep yourself from idols," he was urging them to stay *on alert* regarding the danger of idolatry. In Greek, the word "from" is the word *apo*, which means *from* or *away from*, and in this particular verse it implies *intentional distance*. Thus, John was saying, "Be very intentional about putting space between you and idols." To this command, he added the word "amen," which means *amen; so let it be*. It was an emphasis marker used to emphasize a statement of great importance.

Taking into account the original Greek meanings of these words, here is the *Renner Interpretive Version (RIV)* of First John 5:21:

> **Little children, I immediately order you to withdraw from idols. Those idols — and what they represent — are so evil that you need to seriously guard yourself against them and stay away from them altogether. I'm leaving no wiggle room on this issue. I'm absolutely and emphatically ordering you to immediately put as much space as possible between yourself and idols.**

They are evil and represent a menace to your life, so you must urgently guard against them. What I'm telling you right now is not open for debate and is not optional. It is an order that I fully expect you to obey. In fact, to underscore the seriousness of what I am telling you, I'm even adding an "amen" to stress the point. I expect you to explicitly obey my instructions on this issue — and do it now!

Paganism Abounded in the Ancient World

During the First Century, the world was filled with pagan temples and pagan celebrations. It is impossible to exaggerate the role that pagan temples and idols played in the ancient world. For example…

- The city of **Ephesus** was built around the great Temple of Artemis.
- The city of **Smyrna** was built around the worship of the goddess Cybele.
- The city of **Pergamum** was built around the worship of Zeus and Asclepius.
- The city of **Thyatira** was built around the worship of the god Apollo.
- The city of **Sardis** was built around a great temple to Artemis.
- The city of **Philadelphia** was built around the Temple of Dionysus.
- The city of **Laodicea** was built around the worship of Zeus.
- The city of **Athens** was built around the worship of Athena.
- And the city of **Corinth** was built around the worship of Aphrodite.

These cities and many others were pagan environments entrenched in pagan practices and celebrations. Magic, incantations, amulets, charms, sacrifices, ritual, pagan festivals — all of these were a part of life for all pagans. So living in close quarters with the demonic realm was a daily reality for every believer living in the First Century. BUT there is no record in the book of Acts of preachers, apostles, or believers attending pagan temples to meet people, advertise their messages, help them identify with local populations, or become more "seeker-friendly" to the unchurched.

God called people *out of* those dark environments into His holy community. There was never an option to remain in both worlds — Christ demanded complete *separation* from their pagan past. God called them *out of* darkness *into* His marvelous light (*see* First Peter 2:9). He knew that skirting around the edges of darkness was *not* the way for His children to flourish in His light. A study of idolatry in the Old Testament makes it clear that idolatry is spiritually fatal to God's people. Where idolatry is practiced, evil spiritual floodgates are opened that allow a deluge of moral filth and depravity to pour out.

In New Testament times, we find the same type of warnings against idolatry. The Holy Spirit spoke through Paul and John, telling believers to intentionally put space between themselves and these idolatrous places. Warnings about idolatry are also found throughout the New Testament:

Acts 15:20; Romans 1:22-32; 1 Corinthians 5:5,10; 6:9; 8:1; 10:7,14; Colossians 3:5; 1 Peter 4:3; Revelation 2:14; 9:20; 21:8; 22:15.

All of these passages give strong prohibitions to believers to refrain from involving themselves in pagan practices in pagan environments. Although the Greater One lives in us, we are to use our heads and keep ourselves from demonic-infested environments. Remember, evil is always lurking in the shadows, just waiting for us to drop our guard and fall asleep on the job. So it is essential that we are always on guard — diligent, wide-awake, and doing our part to protect ourselves from the evil that is in the world. A part of being vigilant is to stay away from places, things, or events that are evil — which includes things like Halloween.

We Are To 'Abstain From Pollutions of Idols'

When we come to Acts 15, we see the Early Church leadership convening to discuss what to expect of the Gentile converts who were coming into the Church in large numbers. The conclusion that they came to is recorded in Acts 15:19 and 20: "Wherefore my sentence is, that we trouble not them, which from among the Gentiles are turned to God: but that we write unto them, that they abstain from pollutions of idols...."

Notice the phrase "abstain from." It is the Greek word *apechomai*, which means *to abstain*; *to withdraw from*; *to stay away from*; or *to put distance between oneself and something else*. It carries the idea of *deliberately or intentionally refraining from something*. Furthermore, it indicates *putting physical distance between oneself and another person, place, or thing*. Clearly, "abstaining" is a very intentional action.

Specifically, the apostles said believers are to abstain from "pollutions," which is the Greek word *alisgema*, and it depicts *something that is defiled*. This word makes it clear that *idolatry has a spiritually polluting and contaminating effect* — not because the idol itself is something significant, but because of the demonic powers it represents and that are attracted to the environments where they're worshiped.

This brings us to the word "idols," which is the Greek word *eidolon*. It is plural and indicates *idols of false gods*. Pagan temples were demonic strongholds. Hence, it was imperative for believers to stay away from these places that were saturated with spiritually poisonous activities. There were evil powers there that could have influenced or oppressed their souls. Remember, many of these believers had been delivered from these places of idolatry, and they didn't need to keep going back into them.

It's no wonder that Jesus was so opposed to people like the Nicolaitans who had infiltrated the churches in Ephesus and Pergamum during the First Century. They suggested things like, "Why not burn a little incense to the gods? Why not participate in pagan feasts with your community if it will make your life a little easier?" Jesus hated this doctrine of compromise and forewarned He was going to come quickly to deal with compromisers if they didn't repent.

Shield Yourself and Your Family From Evil Spiritual Influences

Clearly, Jesus' zeal left a mark on the apostle John and motivated him to write First John 5:21, which says, "Little children, keep yourselves from idols. Amen." Again, taking into account the original Greek meaning, here is the *Renner Interpretive Version (RIV)* of First John 5:21:

> **Little children, I immediately order you to withdraw from idols. Those idols — and what they represent — are so evil that you need to seriously guard yourself against them and stay away from them altogether. I'm leaving no wiggle room on this issue. I'm absolutely and emphatically ordering you to immediately put as much space as possible between yourself and idols. They are evil and represent a menace to your life, so you must urgently guard against them. What I'm telling you right now is not open for debate and is not optional. It is an order that I fully expect you to obey. In fact, to underscore the seriousness**

of what I am telling you, I'm even adding an "amen" to stress the point. I expect you to explicitly obey my instructions on this issue — and do it now!"

Now take this verse and apply it to the context of Halloween. How do you think God feels about Christians dressing their children and their grandchildren — and even themselves — in costumes that resemble witches, devils, and other grotesque creatures? How can we teach our children to take the devil's existence seriously and exercise authority over him when we are dressing them like him?

Friend, use your head and listen to the voice of the Holy Spirit when it comes to celebrating Halloween. Don't be afraid of what your family, friends, or neighbors might think of you. Your children and grandchildren are your responsibility, and it is up to you to protect, guard, and shield yourself and them from the evil spiritual influences of this world.

Remember, Colossians 3:17 says, "And whatsoever ye do in word or deed, do all in the name of the Lord Jesus...." Whatever you cannot do in the name of Jesus, you shouldn't do — period. In our next lesson, we are going to examine the history of Halloween and uncover its roots of paganism.

STUDY QUESTIONS

Study to shew thyself approved unto God, a workman that needeth not to be ashamed, rightly dividing the word of truth.
— 2 Timothy 2:15

1. What clear instructions does God give us in Second Corinthians 6:14-18 about who we hang out with? (*See also* First Corinthians 15:33.)

2. One of the reasons for this command is because of *what* we are. What does the Bible call you in First Corinthians 3:16? (*See also* First Corinthians 6:19 and Ephesians 2:22.) If you obey these instructions, what does God promise to do for you?

3. What specific direction does Paul give about keeping company with people practicing idolatry and sexual immorality in First Corinthians 5:9-13? According to First Corinthians 5:1-8, what are we to do with people caught up in these activities? Why is this so important? (*See* First Corinthians 5:6,7.)

PRACTICAL APPLICATION

> But be ye doers of the word, and not hearers only,
> deceiving your own selves.
> — James 1:22

1. In Colossians 3:17 (*NKJV*), God said, "And whatever you do in word or deed, do all in the name of the Lord Jesus...." Stop for a moment and think: *Can I dress my kids (or grandkids) as witches, devils, ghosts, or some other gory creature and do it in the name of Jesus? Can I go to haunted houses and participate in scaring people and bring God glory? Do I have God's blessing to take part in Halloween?*

2. If your answer is no, then you shouldn't do it. What might be a healthy, God-honoring alternative for you and your children or grandchildren to do? What new family traditions might you — and other families — start engaging in that are peaceful, safe, and fun?

LESSON 4

TOPIC

The History of Halloween

SCRIPTURES

1. **1 John 5:21** — Little children, keep yourselves from idols. Amen.

2. **Hosea 4:6** — My people are destroyed for lack of knowledge...

3. **Colossians 3:17** — And whatsoever ye do in word or deed, do all in the name of the Lord Jesus, giving thanks to God and the Father by him.

GREEK WORDS

1. "amen" — ἀμήν (*amen*): amen; so let it be; an emphasis marker used to emphasize a statement of great importance

SYNOPSIS

When it comes to idol worship and pagan celebrations, the citizens of Ephesus didn't need anyone to teach them. In New Testament times, they had erected a massive pagan temple dedicated to Artemis, the goddess of fertility. Inside that temple stood a colossal statue of Artemis, a throng of pagan worshipers, and 6,000 priests and priestesses who served this dark demonic deity around the clock.

Today, the place where the Temple of Artemis once stood is a virtual swampland filled with broken stones. The worship of Artemis was killed by the preaching of the Gospel. Believers in the First Century were taught to stay away from places of idolatry and pagan worship — a message we need to hear and take to heart today.

In our first lesson, we learned that there is nothing funny about the devil; he is a dangerous adversary that must be taken seriously. In Lesson 2, we heard how Early Christians refrained from participating in pagan celebrations. And in Lesson 3, we saw from the Scriptures that as believers we are to avoid participating in pagan events such as Halloween.

The emphasis of this lesson:

The history of Halloween is deeply rooted in the occult and dates back thousands of years to a specific pagan festival that was a celebration of necromancy, which is fellowshipping with the dead. Wearing masks, carving jack-o-lanterns, and burning bonfires all have their origin in this sinister holiday, and their meaning today is quite different than their original intent.

A Review of Our Anchor Verse

First John 5:21 says, "Little children, keep yourselves from idols. Amen." We have seen that the word "keep" is the Greek word *phulasso*, which basically means *to protect yourself, to guard yourself, or to shield yourself from something*. It carries the idea *to guard, to protect, to secure, to shield, or watch over in order to protect one from some outside foul force*. The tense of the word *phulasso* here doesn't refer to a temporary alertness, but rather *a lifelong determination to remain wide-awake and on course to the very end*.

John's use of this word in the context of idolatry and pagan celebrations conveys that *we are to guard, to protect, to preserve, and to shield ourselves* from places and practices of idolatry. When John charged his readers to "...keep yourself from idols," he was urging them to stay *on alert* regarding the danger of idolatry. In Greek, the word "from" is the word *apo*, and in this case it implies *intentional distance*. Thus, John was saying, "Be very intentional about putting distance between you and idols — or anything that is evil." To this command, he added the word "amen," which means *amen; so let it be. It is an emphasis marker used to emphasize a statement of great importance.*

Taking into account the original Greek meanings, here is the *Renner Interpretive Version (RIV)* of First John 5:21:

> **Little children, I immediately order you to withdraw from idols. Those idols — and what they represent — are so evil that you need to seriously guard yourself against them and stay away from them altogether. I'm leaving no wiggle room on this issue. I'm absolutely and emphatically ordering you to immediately put as much space as possible between yourself and idols. They are evil and represent a menace to your life, so you must urgently guard against them. What I'm telling you right now is not open for debate and is not optional. It is an order that I fully expect you to obey. In fact, to underscore the seriousness of what I am telling you, I'm even adding an "amen" to stress the point. I expect you to explicitly obey my instructions on this issue — and do it now!"**

How Do You Remember Celebrating Halloween?

Every year, people all over the world celebrate Halloween — including numerous Christians. For many, the festivities start in the beginning of October as people post scary images in their windows and on their front doors. Some individuals turn their lawns into realistic graveyards, while others convert their porches into haunted scenes, featuring life-sized coffins, stuffed figures, and stretched-out spider webbing.

In schools, Halloween crafts are interwoven throughout the children's activities. Teachers distribute coloring pages for students to decorate, featuring images of jack-o-lanterns, witches, vampires, and mummies. Ghosts, goblins, and bats created from construction paper are tied to strings and hung around the classroom. The frenzy of fright builds right up to the fateful night of October 31. Even before the sun has fully set, children take to the streets dressed in a wide assortment of costumes ranging from superheroes and princesses to the most grotesque creatures ever seen. It is estimated that in the United States alone, more than 150 million to 175 million Americans participate in Halloween, spending between $8 billion to $9 billion annually.

Halloween parties and haunted houses are also a popular activity throughout the season — even in churches. Rick shared how he grew up in a Christian home with loving parents who led him to the Lord and taught him the Word of God. Yet they participated in Halloween every year. They, like many Christians, simply didn't have a revelation about the devil or the evil, pagan roots of the celebration. This confirms what God said in Hosea 4:6: "My people are destroyed for lack of knowledge…." Once we truly understand the history behind Halloween and the element of evil behind it, we are much less likely to engage in its festivities.

The History of Halloween

The celebration of Halloween, which falls on October 31, dates back thousands of years to a specific pagan festival. The word "pagan" describes one who is an idolater, a heathen, or an unbeliever. The pagans who celebrated this holiday believed that on October 31 the veil between the worlds of the living and the dead was the thinnest, and at that time the dead could pass back through that veil and walk where they had walked before they died.

This Celtic pagan festival — which eventually became known as Halloween — was a celebration of *necromancy*, which is communicating and fellowshipping with the dead. Pagans believed that those who died in the previous year, and who had not yet moved on, could interact with the living. The truth is, the people who practice this dark divination are not actually contacting people who have departed; they are tapping into the spirit realm and connecting with demonic spirits that are familiar with the person they are trying to reach.

The Origin of Bonfires: Early Christian leaders described this celebration as dark, evil, and sinister. As part of the festivities, cattle were slaughtered and sacrificed and their bones were put into "bone fires" — which came to be known as "bonfires." These activities were carried out in an effort to communicate with the dead. Again, these pagans believed that October 31 was a time when the "thin line" between the natural-realm and the spirit-realm evaporated and otherworldly visitors would show up in the realm of the living. Departed loved ones were expected – and welcomed. The pagan's belief was so strong they even set out the favorite foods of those who had died. Again, this is necromancy, and it is still practiced in many parts of the world today.

The Origin of Costumes: Sometimes when spirits appeared, they took the form of monsters and evil beings. It was believed that a dead person, who had been wronged by someone still living, could come back to torture them. To guard themselves from being recognized by those spirits, people darkened their faces with ashes from the bonfires to disguise themselves — a practice that later became known as "guising." This disguising eventually developed over time into wearing masks.

History documents that the Catholic Church turned October 31 into "All-Hallowed Eve," making it a night of prayer to remember the martyrs of the Church who had been slain for their faith. But the old pagan ways simply would not die out. The bonfires continued, and the celebration of Halloween was eventually brought to America in the mid-1800s.

The Origin of Jack-O-Lanterns: When it comes to Halloween, carved pumpkins — or jack-o-lanterns — are icons most people think about. This tradition was based on the folk tale of "Stingy Jack" — a drunk con-man who fooled the devil into banning him from hell. But because of his sinful life, he couldn't enter heaven either. The story concludes that after his death, his departed spirit began roaming the earth, carrying a turnip that had been hallowed out and carved with the face of a jack-o-lantern. Inside the turnip, a red-hot ember from hell had been placed to light his way through eternal darkness. So on the night of October 31 — when the veil between life and death was believed to be the thinnest — people began carving jack-o-lanterns, inserting candles inside them, and placing them on their front porch. They believed the lighted jack-o-lanterns would protect them from evil spirits that passed into the natural-realm and roamed the earth seeking revenge.

Modern Pagans and Witches: Many Neo-pagans and Wiccans (witches) in our day continue to celebrate Halloween as closely as possible to how it was first celebrated thousands of years ago. For them, it is a high holy day for paganism and witchcraft. Still to this day, the central theme is that moment on October 31, when they believe the veil between the spirit realm and natural realm is the thinnest, and as a result, they can interact with the dead by luring them to cross over into the land of the living.

Again, these Neo-pagans and Wiccans are not interacting with the actual people who passed away; they are communicating with demonic spirits that have disguised themselves as other entities — and those entities might even appear as people that once lived. Furthermore, Neo-pagans and Wiccans (witches) still slaughter animals and burn their bones in the flames of "bone-fires."

Make no mistake: Halloween — from its very beginning — is evil. The entire event is designed to open a door to a dark spiritual-realm. That is what occult activities are — they are door-openers to the spirit-realm. There is nothing funny about these activities and they are actually quite dangerous.

In light of all this history, here are seven questions you need to ask yourself and answer honestly:

1. Would Jesus dress like the *devil* to celebrate Halloween?
2. Would Jesus dress like a *witch* to celebrate Halloween?
3. Would Jesus dress like a *ghost* to celebrate Halloween?
4. Would Jesus find demons or witchcraft *entertaining*?
5. Would Jesus' apostles encourage Christians to celebrate pagan feasts?
6. Would Early New Testament Christians throw parties around evil entities?
7. Would the Holy Spirit want you to bring Him into the dark, pagan celebration of Halloween?

If your answer to these seven questions is "no," then why would you celebrate it? Remember, Colossians 3:17 says, "And whatsoever ye do in word or deed, do all in the name of the Lord Jesus, giving thanks to God and the Father by him." If you cannot participate in and celebrate Halloween in the name of the Lord Jesus — believing He is pleased and approves of all your actions — then you shouldn't be involved in it.

Looking once more at the original Greek meaning, here is the *Renner Interpretive Version (RIV)* of First John 5:21:

> **Little children, I immediately order you to withdraw from idols. Those idols — and what they represent — are so evil that you need to seriously guard yourself against them and stay away from them altogether. I'm leaving no wiggle room on this issue. I'm absolutely and emphatically ordering you to immediately put as much space as possible between yourself and idols. They are evil and represent a menace to your life, so you must**

urgently guard against them. What I'm telling you right now is not open for debate and is not optional. It is an order that I fully expect you to obey. In fact, to underscore the seriousness of what I am telling you, I'm even adding an "amen" to stress the point. I expect you to explicitly obey my instructions on this issue — and do it now!"

A careful look at this verse answers all seven of the previous questions.

An Important Point of History

During the First Century, Timothy served as the pastor of the church of Ephesus, and he held that position for many years. One day there was a huge pagan celebration that took place on the nearby street of Curetes — the most ancient street in Ephesus. This celebration was the equivalent of what we would call Halloween. As the pagans came marching down the street, they were dressed in all kinds of costumes and carried long poles with images or figurines attached to the top.

History records that when Pastor Timothy saw the ungodly display parading down the street, he barged out on to where they were and began rebuking them. With great boldness, he told them to take off their masks and lay down their effigies, but the pagans didn't listen. Instead, they began to beat him to death with their poles. That is how Timothy was killed — during the equivalent of a Halloween celebration right in the heart of Ephesus.

What is most remarkable about this story is the fearlessness Timothy displayed. Earlier in his life, he had battled with fear, which is why Paul wrote to him and said, "For God hath not given us the spirit of fear; but of power, and of love, and of a sound mind" (2 Timothy 1:7). The Holy Spirit had so worked in Timothy's life that in the end he truly was "as bold as a lion" (see Proverbs 28:1).

In our final lesson, we will look at some specific Bible verses regarding the occult and how occult activities are "door-openers" to an evil and dark spiritual realm.

STUDY QUESTIONS

**Study to shew thyself approved unto God, a workman that
needeth not to be ashamed, rightly dividing the word of truth.
— 2 Timothy 2:15**

First John 5:21, says, "Little children, keep yourselves from idols. Amen."
Take a few moments to meditate on the Amplified version of this verse:
"Little children, keep yourselves from idols (false gods) — [from anything
and everything that would occupy the place in your heart due to God,
from any sort of substitute for Him that would take first place in your
life]. Amen (so let it be)."

1. What is the Holy Spirit speaking to you through this verse?

2. In light of how it defines *idols*, do you have anything in your life that
    is trying to occupy the place in your heart that is due to God? Is there
    any person, place, or thing you are knowingly or unknowingly substi-
    tuting for Him and allowing to take first place in your life? If so, what
    is it?

3. What specific actions is the Holy Spirit prompting you to take to
    "keep" yourself from these idols and break off all fellowship with
    them?

PRACTICAL APPLICATION

**But be ye doers of the word, and not hearers only,
deceiving your own selves.
— James 1:22**

1. Looking back at your childhood, how do you remember celebrating
    Halloween? Did you decorate your home or visit haunted houses? Did
    you dress up in costumes and go trick-or-treating?

2. Of all the historical facts presented in this lesson, what was the most
    sobering and eye-opening? Why? After hearing all that you heard,
    how has it impacted your desire to let your kids or grandkids partici-
    pate in celebrating Halloween?

TOPIC

How Should You Respond to Halloween?

SCRIPTURES

1. **1 John 5:21** — Little children, keep yourselves from idols. Amen.

2. **Deuteronomy 18:9-12 (*NKJV*)**— When you come into the land which the LORD your God is giving you, you shall not learn to follow the abominations of those nations. There shall not be found among you *anyone* who makes his son or his daughter pass through the fire [an ancient occult practice], or *one* who practices witchcraft, *or* a soothsayer, or one who interprets omens, or a sorcerer, or one who conjures spells, or a medium, or a spiritist, or one who calls up the dead. For all who do these things *are* an abomination [detestable] to the Lord…

3. **Isaiah 47:10-14 (*NKJV*)** — For you have trusted in your wickedness… Therefore evil shall come upon you… trouble shall fall upon you… Let now the astrologers, the stargazers, and the monthly prognosticators stand up and save you from what shall come upon you. Behold, they shall be as stubble, The fire shall burn them; They shall not deliver themselves from the power of the flame…

4. **Revelation 21:8 (*NIV*)** — …Those who practice magic arts…[their place will be in] the fiery lake of burning sulfur. This is the second death.

5. **1 Corinthians 10:13,14** — There hath no temptation taken you but such as is common to man: but God is faithful, who will not suffer you to be tempted above that ye are able; but will with the temptation also make a way to escape, that ye may be able to bear it. Wherefore, my dearly beloved, flee from idolatry.

GREEK WORDS

1. "escape" ἔκβασις (*ekbasis*): in context, to get up, use your feet, and remove yourself from a situation that isn't good for you; to walk out

of a difficult place; to remove yourself from a person or place that isn't good for you; to use your feet to exit a situation or environment

2. "flee" — **φεύγω** (*pheugo*): to flee, to take flight, to run away, to run hastily, to run as fast as possible, or to escape; pictures one's feet flying as he runs from a situation

3. "amen" — **ἀμήν** (*amen*): amen; so let it be; an emphasis marker used to emphasize a statement of great importance

4. "taken" — **λαμβάνω** (*lambano*): to seize; to attack; to grip; or to take hold of

5. "common to man" — **ἀνθρώπινος** (*anthropinos*): anything commonly experienced by human beings; unexceptional; merely human

6. "tempted" — **πειράζω** (*peirasmos*): an intense examination; a fiery trial or experience

7. "above" — **ὑπέρ** (*huper*): something that is above and beyond; excessive; implies something unbearable or beyond one's ability to overcome

8. "make" — **ποιέω** (*poieo*): where we get the word poet; future tense, and means will creatively make a way

SYNOPSIS

As we have noted throughout this study, the ancient city of Ephesus was home to the great Temple of Artemis, one of the seven wonders of the ancient world. The apostle Paul, along with the help of Aquila and Priscilla, worked to establish a powerful church in Ephesus — one that would become known for training and sending out missionaries to other parts of the world.

Everywhere Paul went, he taught believers not to go near pagan temples. Specifically, he urged them to "...flee from idolatry" (1 Corinthians 10:14). We saw that the word "flee" is a Greek word that pictures *moving your feet as fast as you can to get out of a situation*. Believers learned to flee, not because they were afraid of the devil, but because they understood that pagan temples were filled with demonic activity, and they knew better than to subject themselves to that bad spiritual influence.

This brings us to the celebration of Halloween. Should Christians be participating in this pagan event? Clearly, there is nothing funny about the devil. He is a thief who comes to steal, kill, and destroy, and Halloween is a pagan celebration that opens the door to demonic activity. As believers, we should seek to put space between ourselves and such ungodly activities. Although this may be a new way of thinking for you, it is good spiritual common sense that could save you and your family from considerable trouble.

The emphasis of this lesson:

The occult is man's attempt to tap into the spirit-realm or obtain insights about the future without God's assistance. There are hundreds of occult practices, many of which are directly connected with the events of Halloween. God's Word clearly warns us again and again to abstain from every form of occult activities as they are an abomination in God's sight.

A Summary of Our Anchor Verse

Turning our attention to First John 5:21, it says, "Little children, keep yourselves from idols. Amen." We have seen that the word "keep" is the Greek word *phulasso*, which basically means *to protect yourself, guard yourself, or shield yourself from something*. In this case, we are *to guard, to protect*, and *to shield* ourselves from "idols" — which means any *false gods*. The tense of the word *phulasso* here doesn't refer to a temporary alertness, but rather *a lifelong determination to remain wide-awake and on course to the very end*.

When John said, "...Keep yourself from idols," the word "from" is the Greek word *apo*, and in this verse it implies *intentional distance*. Hence, he is urging us to be very intentional about putting distance between us and anything that is spiritually evil.

Taking into account the original Greek meanings, here is the *Renner Interpretive Version (RIV)* of First John 5:21:

> **Little children, I immediately order you to withdraw from idols. Those idols — and what they represent — are so evil that you need to seriously guard yourself against them and stay away from them altogether. I'm leaving no wiggle room on this issue. I'm absolutely and emphatically ordering you to immediately put as much space as possible between yourself and idols. They are evil and represent a menace to your life, so you must urgently guard against them. What I'm telling you right now is not open for debate and is not optional. It is an order that I**

fully expect you to obey. In fact, to underscore the seriousness of what I am telling you, I'm even adding an "amen" to stress the point. I expect you to explicitly obey my instructions on this issue — and do it now!"

Timothy Stood Valiantly Against Paganism

At the close of the last lesson, we noted that during the First Century, Timothy was serving as the senior pastor of the church of Ephesus, and Ephesus was a very dark, pagan city. From time to time, there would be extravagant pagan celebrations that took place in the city. On one such occasion, a large band of pagans began parading down the nearby street of Curetes — one of the oldest sections in the city. These pagans were dressed in costumes and carrying long poles with images or effigies attached to the top. It was a celebration very similar to what we would call Halloween.

Knowing how events like this attracted demonic activity, Pastor Timothy barged out onto the street where the pagans were marching and began rebuking them. With great boldness, he told them to take off their masks, lay down their effigies, and repent, but they didn't listen. Instead, they began to beat Timothy to death with their poles and effigies. History records that is how he died — he was beaten to death by pagans during the equivalent of a Halloween celebration right in the heart of Ephesus.

Earlier in Timothy's life, he was battling with fear, which is why Paul wrote him and said, "For God hath not given us the spirit of fear; but of power, and of love, and of a sound mind" (2 Timothy 1:7). Clearly, when Timothy confronted the pagans, he was fearless. The Holy Spirit had so worked in Timothy's life that in the end he truly was "as bold as a lion" (*see* Proverbs 28:1).

A Sampling of Occult Activities

The word "occult" is generally associated with "secret knowledge" and with occult practices designed to interact with supernatural phenomenon from the spirit-realm. Occult activities are designed to give you information and knowledge that you would normally receive from God — either in His Word or through His Spirit. Thus, the occult is man's attempt to obtain insights about the future or access the spirit-realm without the assistance of God.

Although there are hundreds of occult practices, here are a few more notable ones forbidden by Scripture — some of which are directly related to the festivities of Halloween:

- **Astrology** – seeking direction for one's life from signs and patterns in the stars.
- **Automatic speaking** – opening your mouth and allowing spirits to speak through you.
- **Automatic writing** – placing a pen in your hand and allowing spirits to guide you in writing.
- **Calling up the dead** – conjuring up those who have passed away.
- **Channeling** – a modern-day term for a medium.
- **Chiromancy** – another name for reading palms.
- **Clairaudience** – similar to clairvoyance; perceiving by hearing the inaudible voices of spirits.
- **Clairvoyance** – a form of divining, telepathy, of fortune telling.
- **Crystallomancy** – determining one's future through the use of crystals and crystal ball.
- **Demon worship** and **consultation**.
- **Divination** – predicting and prophesying the future; Balaam was involved in divination.
- **Enchantments** – using magic and charms to determine one's future.
- **Fortune telling** – the forecasting of one's future.
- **Horoscopes** – seeking to know one's future through the study of the zodiac.
- **Incantations** – using verbal chants, invocations, prayers, or spells to connect with spirits.
- **Mediums** – someone who acts as a go-between to connect someone with a person who died.
- **Mirror gazing** – staring into mirrors in order to determine one's future.
- **Necromancy** – flirting or fellowshipping with the dead (what Halloween clearly is about).

- **Omens** – forecasting one's future through the use of signs, warnings, and premonitions.
- **Oracles** – an answer/decision allegedly given by an ancient deity speaking through someone.
- **Ouija boards** – a game where an amulet moves by the power of evil spirits telling the future.
- **Palmistry** – telling one's future through palm-reading.
- **Prognostication** – a form of predicting the future through divination and soothsaying.
- **Psychometry** – a type of divination using an object to find facts about an object or its owner.
- **Scrying** – attempting to determine one's future by looking at the entrails of dead animals.
- **Soothsaying** – another name for fortune-telling, mysticism, or clairvoyance.
- **Sorcery** – tapping into the spirit-realm using black magic, witchcraft, necromancy, etc.
- **Spells** (casting and conjuring) – a spoken word or words believed to have magic power.
- **Spirit-guides** – a disembodied spirit that is believed to guide or protect someone living.
- **Spiritists** – a belief that one can speak with or on behalf of the spirits of the dead.
- **Tarot cards** – attempting to determine one's future through the use of special cards.
- **Teacup reading** – a form of fortune-telling by gazing into tea-filled cups.
- **Wicca** – another name for witch/wizard; belief in male and female deities existing in nature.
- **Witchcraft** – the use of sorcery or magic; communication with the devil or evil spirits.
- **Wizardry** – use of sorcery, witchcraft, conjuring, magic, necromancy, enchantments, etc.

All of these are occult practices, and they are clearly forbidden in Scripture. People have used them — and still use them — to gain access into the spirit-realm and to get answers regarding their future. But every one of these activities is man's attempt to gain secret knowledge apart from God and His Word. When a person seeks wisdom through these avenues, they open a doorway to a dark, sinister spiritual realm that will invade their life.

Scripture Clearly Forbids Involvement in the Occult

The Bible is filled with clear warnings about staying away from occult practices.

Deuteronomy 18:9 and 10 (*NKJV*) says, "When you come into the land which the Lord your God is giving you, you shall not learn to follow the abominations of those nations. There shall not be found among you anyone who makes his son or his daughter pass through the fire [an ancient occult practice], or one who practices witchcraft, or a soothsayer, or one who interprets omens, or a sorcerer, or one who conjures spells, or a medium, or a spiritist, or one who calls up the dead. For all who do these things are an abomination [detestable] to the Lord...."

There are nine specific occult practices God lists in this passage, and He calls them an *abomination*.

In **Isaiah 47:10-14 (*NKJV*)**, God said, "...For you have trusted in your wickedness... Therefore evil shall come upon you... trouble shall fall upon you... Let now the astrologers, the stargazers, and the monthly prognosticators stand up and save you from these things that shall come upon you. Behold, they shall be as stubble, the fire shall burn them; they shall not deliver themselves from the power of the flame..."

In this passage, three additional occult practices are mentioned, including *astrology*. Unlike astronomy, which is a general study of the stars and the planets, *astrology* is predicting the future by the movement and alignment of planets, stars, or the moon. It includes the use of horoscopes and is sometimes referred to as "observing times" in the Old Testament. God hates this.

Revelation 21:8 (*NIV*) talks about another major category of the occult, declaring "...Those who practice magic arts ...their place will be in the fiery lake of burning sulfur. This is the second death." When the Bible talks about *magic arts*, it is referring to divination, channeling, charming, clairvoyance, enchantments, familiar spirits, fortune telling, magic, mediums, necromancy, séances, sorcery, spells, spiritism, spirit-guides, wizardry, and witchcraft. God condemns all these things and says those who practice them have a place in the lake of fire.

What other occult practices does the Bible specifically alert us to stay away from? Not consulting mediums and spiritists is a recurring theme. **First Chronicles 10:13 and 14** reveal that King Saul died because he consulted a medium for guidance. Warnings against these forbidden activities can also be found in **Isaiah 8:19; Deuteronomy 18:9-14; Isaiah 44:25; Jeremiah 27:9; Second Kings 21:6** and **23:24.**

Then when you come to **Ezekiel 21:21, Isaiah 19:3**, and **First Samuel 28**, the Bible clearly states that divination and spiritism are despised, dark, evil forbidden practices. In **Daniel 2:27** the Bible says those who claim to have the ability to predict the future based on their powers — or the powers of spirits — are unable to do so correctly. We're also told in **Ezekiel 13:8, Jeremiah 14:14**, and **Isaiah 44:25** that those who practice divination are deceivers filled with nonsense and lies.

To be clear, God's abhorrence of mediums is intense. In **Leviticus 19:31** the Bible says a medium or a spiritist living among God's people was actually a spiritual defilement. And in **Leviticus 20:27**, He stated that if a medium was found in the camp of the Israelites, that person was to be executed. Are you getting the notion of what Scripture is saying?

God Promises You a 'Way To Escape'

First Century believers living in Corinth were presented with a challenging situation. At that time, the best cuts of meat were only available inside of pagan temples. Pagans brought meat offerings and sacrificed them to the gods. The pagan priests would then sell the meat to the people in the community. Therefore, in order to buy good meat, believers had to expose themselves to the ungodly atmosphere of the pagan temples and the vile activities taking place inside. By the time they exited the pagan temple, many of these believers were back under the influence of demon spirits.

To effectively put a stop to this demonic influence, the apostle Paul encouraged the Corinthian believers not to eat meat offered to idols. He then said, "There hath no temptation taken you but such as is common to man: but God is faithful, who will not suffer you to be tempted above that ye are able; but will with the temptation also make a way to escape, that ye may be able to bear it" (1 Corinthians 10:13).

There are several important words in this verse, starting with the word "taken." It is the Greek word *lambano*, which means *to seize; to attack; to grip*; or *to take hold of*. Paul said, "There is no temptation that has *seized you, attacked you*, or *taken hold of you* that is not "common to man." In Greek, the phrase "common to man" is *anthropinos*, and it means *anything commonly experienced by human beings; unexceptional; merely human*.

Paul went on to say that God "…will not suffer you to be tempted above that ye are able…" (1 Corinthians 10:13). The word "tempted" is the Greek word *peirasmos*, which describes *an intense examination; a fiery trial or experience*. Paul said that God won't permit you to experience a fiery trial or experience that is "above" what you can bear. The word "above" is the Greek word *huper*, and it describes *something that is above and beyond; excessive*. In this instance, it implies *something unbearable or beyond one's ability to overcome*.

With every temptation, Paul assured us that God would "…make a way to escape, that ye may be able to bear it" (1 Corinthians 10:13). The word "make" is the Greek word *poieo*, which is from where we get the word *poet*. In this case, it is a future tense and means *will creatively make a way* to "escape." The Greek word for "escape" is *ekbasis*, which means *to get up, use your feet, and remove yourself from a situation that isn't good for you*. It depicts *walking out of a difficult place* or *to remove yourself from a person or place that isn't good for you*. The implication is to use your feet to exit a situation or environment and put distance between you and that evil thing.

With his next breath, the apostle Paul urgently warned, "Wherefore, my dearly beloved, flee from idolatry" (1 Corinthians 10:14). We saw in Lesson 2 that the word "flee" here is the Greek word *pheugo*, which means *to flee, to take flight, to run away, to run hastily, to run as fast as possible, or to escape*. It pictures one's feet flying as he runs from a situation. The tense used here conveys they were to *constantly flee* from idolatry with no exception. By using this word, Paul was emphatically stating that idolatry and pagan celebrations are so fatal, they should never be tolerated under any circumstances.

By going to pagan temples that were ripe with sexual immorality and demonic activity, the Corinthian believers put themselves in a bad position. Although an idol by itself is nothing, the environment in which idolatry and pagan activities are practiced is *permeated* with demonic activity. That is why Paul told them to avoid places of temptation.

Friend, if you know evil is trying to suck you in, get up, get moving, and get out of there before it traps you! Lightning bolts and angelic appearances are not likely to occur to show you the way out. Flee from the temptation — *move your feet as fast as you can and get out of there!* Your greatest way of escape is using your two feet.

This brings us back, one last time, to our anchor verse in First John 5:21: "Little children, keep yourselves from idols. Amen." Taking into account the original Greek meanings, here is the *Renner Interpretive Version (RIV)* of First John 5:21:

Little children, I immediately order you to withdraw from idols. Those idols — and what they represent — are so evil that you need to seriously guard yourself against them and stay away from them altogether. I'm leaving no wiggle room on this issue. I'm absolutely and emphatically ordering you to immediately put as much space as possible between yourself and idols. They are evil and represent a menace to your life, so you must urgently guard against them. What I'm telling you right now is not open for debate and is not optional. It is an order that I fully expect you to obey. In fact, to underscore the seriousness of what I am telling you, I'm even adding an "amen" to stress the point. I expect you to explicitly obey my instructions on this issue — and do it now!"

The *Renner Interpretive Version (RIV)* of First John 5:21, along with all that we have studied in this series, should answer the question of how you should respond to Halloween — an event that is directly related to necromancy and rooted in the occult. If you want to close the door to the devil and the demonic activity connected with Halloween, you need to distance yourself from participating in the event. Instead, join together with other Christian families and develop a healthy alternative celebration. This could include praise and worship, prayer, as well as sharing good wholesome fellowship and food. By celebrating God's goodness, you'll open the door to His glorious presence in your life and invite His blessing.

STUDY QUESTIONS

Study to shew thyself approved unto God, a workman that needeth
not to be ashamed, rightly dividing the word of truth.
— 2 Timothy 2:15

1. When it comes to evil, God's Word says, "Let your way in life be far from her, and come not near the door of her house [avoid the very scenes of temptation]" (Proverbs 5:8 *AMPC*). What are some specific "scenes of temptation" you know in your heart you need to stay away from — sinful issues or habits you've struggled with in the past that the enemy has used to imprison you?

2. What are you presently doing to distance yourself from these places, people, or activities? If what you are doing is *not* working, pray and ask the Holy Spirit to reveal a divine strategy for placing space between you and the "scenes of temptation."

3. Sometimes we will find ourselves in a tempting situation that we didn't see coming and that we had no control over. In those moments, God has promised us to "make a way of escape" (1 Corinthians 10:13). If you find yourself in such a situation, pray and ask God to show you the fastest way to exit the situation and never return.

PRACTICAL APPLICATION

But be ye doers of the word, and not hearers only,
deceiving your own selves.
— James 1:22

1. From all that you've learned in these lessons, why do you believe Christians should avoid celebrating Halloween? What are some quick, specific points you can respectfully share with a friend to encourage them not to participate in this event and create a healthy alternative instead?

2. As you read through the laundry list of occult practices, which ones had you never heard of? Which ones were you familiar with? Have you ever knowingly or unknowingly engaged in any of these activities? If so, which one(ones)?

3. When a person seeks wisdom or power through the occult, they open a doorway to a dark, sinister spiritual realm that will invade their life. If you have dabbled in any form of the occult, God can set you free

from the demonic influence coming against you. Take a few moments to get alone with Him and pray this **prayer of repentance and renunciation**:

Thank You, Father, for revealing this truth to me about participating in pagan practices and activities You call an abomination. Right now I confess and renounce any and all involvement in the occult (name any specific form of the occult the Holy Spirit brings to mind; read back over the list of common practices). *I ask You to forgive me for unknowingly (or knowingly) participating in these things. I abandon my involvement once and for all and ask You to break any curse off my life or the lives of my children and grandchildren. Lord, close any door to the demonic spirit-realm I may have opened. Thank You for hearing and answering my prayer. In Jesus' name, Amen.*